NO REPLY

NO REPLY

A Jewish Child Aboard the MS St. Louis
and the Ordeal That Followed

By Henry Gallant

As Told To Pamela Sampson

Printed in the United States of America
First Printing, 2017
ISBN: 0692812695
ISBN 9780692812693
Library of Congress Control Number: 2017903224
Pamela Sampson, Atlanta,GEORGIA

Ordering Information:
The authors can be contacted on Social Media via LinkedIn,
Facebook or on Twitter at @pamelasampson or @HenryGallantATL
or via email at editorpam@hotmail.com

Dedicated to Mark and Areanna

Preface

THIS BOOK HAS as its origin a lecture held at the William Breman Jewish Heritage Museum in Atlanta, Georgia. On Sunday, May 18, 2014, the guest speaker was Henry Gallant, one of a small number of remaining survivors of the 1939 voyage of the MS St. Louis.

Mr. Gallant was invited to help mark the 75th anniversary of the ship's ill-fated search for safe harbor, recounting the story to a packed audience.

When I learned, after introducing myself to Mr. Gallant, that he had not written his memoirs, I immediately offered to help him do so. As a long-time journalist, I knew a good story when I heard one, and this was one for the ages.

Mr. Gallant was 85 years old when we started. Some details and memories by then had become foggy or lost. But much of the journey he still remembers.

"No Reply: A Jewish Child Aboard the MS St. Louis and the Ordeal That Followed" is the result of our joint effort to preserve a harrowing and necessary story for generations to come.

Acknowledgments

IN WRITING THIS book, I am in the greatest of debt to the historians and scholars of the Holocaust; some are mentioned in the bibliography. Their devotion to the investigation, study and teaching of this epic period of human and inhuman history, and of its vanished people and places, is of irreplaceable value if we are ever to move toward a world where justice, morality and tolerance prevail, and persecution becomes a relic of the past.

— P.S.

When I think of future generations, my guess is that the experience of the Jews during World War II will become a religious thing, perhaps even more than a historical thing, maybe like the Haggadah, the story of Passover, which Jews recite over and over, every year. What we went through was big, and it seems to me that it will grow with the passage of time.

— Henry Gallant

Introduction

IT WAS 1950 — and hardly a better time for America. The rawboned years of World War II had given way to a level of prosperity never known to the average man. The U.S. economy, which had been tightly controlled to serve the war, was now unleashed for the consumer. Chevrolet hardtops and single-family homes replaced Victory Gardens and war bonds as emblems of patriotism. Five years on, America was levitating on the glory of a military victory over Nazism that had saved mankind. Never in history was there such a total triumph of good over evil.

Or had it been? Soon, the world would learn of a parallel war, whose output of slaughter was beyond anything ever seen or imagined. What Winston Churchill called "the most horrible crime ever committed in the whole history of the world" was in sum a colossal hunt-to-kill spree aimed at Europe's millennia-old Jewish community. When concluded, it had claimed the lives of 6 million Jews, including 1 million children. This uniquely evil crime would eventually have its own name: the Holocaust.

Pamela Sampson

Very few survived. Henry Gallant was among those who did. Born in Germany in 1928 to Jewish parents, he spent his youth on the run and ultimately found safety in neutral Switzerland. He spent his formative years there, enrolling in a hotel school and training for a career in hospitality. This gave him skills that he was able to put to use in America after the war. Former GIs didn't want to wait on tables or cook, but Henry didn't mind peeling vegetables or opening doors for guests. He easily found work.

The tony, Renaissance-styled Park Sheraton Hotel across from Carnegie Hall in New York served as a playpen for the rich and famous. Industry barons, mafia dons and movie stars could be seen floating around the gilded lobby or hunkering down in the discreetly lit bar while doormen and waiters bustled across the marble floors like ants.

Henry was hired to operate the Park Sheraton's elevator between the 26th and 31st floors, where the luxury suites for permanent residents like the racy film star Mae West were located. It was exciting for a young Holocaust survivor like Henry to brush up against such moneyed and famous people. But Henry was stunned the first time he found himself face-to-face with one particular resident: Eleanor Roosevelt. She lived on the 31st floor.

Just seeing her provoked troubling memories. In November 1938, when Henry was 10 years old, the systematic persecution of Jews in Germany culminated in

NO REPLY

Kristallnacht — the infamous "Night of Broken Glass" — a frenzy of anti-Semitic violence during which the Nazis burned down or destroyed hundreds of synagogues and Jewish businesses and arrested thousands of Jewish men.

That was when Henry's family decided to leave Germany. They sold their last possessions and bought tickets for the MS St. Louis, an ocean liner set to sail in May 1939 for Cuba, where they hoped to find safety. But when the ship arrived, Cuba's president refused to let the passengers come ashore. The MS St. Louis was ordered out of Cuban waters. So the ship sailed toward Florida. Surely America would help.

The ship got so close to shore that Henry could see the lights off Miami — safety was just a few miles away! Yet the U.S. government would not let the refugees land. Emergency requests for help went all the way to President Franklin D. Roosevelt and Eleanor, his wife, but there was no reply. The ship was forced to return to Europe. Henry and his mother ran from hiding place to hiding place; his father was arrested and transported to face an agonizing fate at Auschwitz.

Undeniably, FDR could have saved them as well as hundreds of other St. Louis passengers who were sent back to Europe and to their deaths. And every time Eleanor Roosevelt entered Henry's elevator, it was as if the soul of his father followed.

This is Henry's story.

CHAPTER 1

I HAVE ONLY an incomplete picture of my father and his family — the uncles, aunts and grandparents who were murdered as part of Hitler's Final Solution and who took with them the memories and legacy of their generation. But one thing is certain: they were loyal and proud Germans and never imagined the betrayal that awaited them.

My grandfather, Salomon Goldstein (known as Saly) was born in Iserlohn in Westphalia, Germany, and eventually settled in the hilly, forested northern town of Herford. Saly's first wife died young, and according to Jewish custom at the time, he was obliged more or less to marry his late wife's sister, Eugenie. So he did, and together, Saly and Eugenie had five sons, all born in Herford; my father was the oldest.

Saly was a livestock veterinarian, which required a lot of stamina and tolerance for manure, fleas and filth. In those days, veterinarians didn't treat dogs and other house pets. They were experts in treating farm animals like cattle and hogs. As I imagine it, he traveled over the Rhineland to help birth calves and tend to sick horses and mules that provided so much of the available transportation for people and goods at the turn of the century.

The Goldstein family was very assimilated. I cannot say one way or the other to what extent they observed the rites of the Jewish religion. They may or may not have avoided pork or lit candles on the Jewish Sabbath each Friday night. What I know for certain is that when it came to identity, the Goldstein family felt German first; to them, Judaism was a bit of an afterthought. Thus when World War I erupted in 1914, my father and his four brothers immediately and enthusiastically enlisted in the German Imperial Army.

My father, Hermann, was a noncommissioned officer. He fought in the infamous Battle of Verdun, a massive German attack on France and one of the longest and bloodiest battles in history. It was fought to a standoff and made Gen. Philippe Pétain a hero in France. For my father's role in Verdun, Germany awarded him the Iron Cross (First Class) for bravery, a medal awarded to only about 5 percent of all soldiers.

It is a fact that our family made the ultimate sacrifice for the German cause. My father's youngest brother, Arthur, was killed in battle — one of 12,000 German-Jewish soldiers who died fighting for the fatherland. He had been a vice-sergeant of the 2nd Infanterie-Regiment 192 and was listed as missing in action on July 4, 1916. The exact circumstances of his death aren't known, but I am sure it was a far easier fate than the one awaiting my father in the next world war.

The Goldstein family. Standing (left to right) are my father; my Aunt Stella and Uncle Walter; Aunt Margarete and Uncle Erwin; Seated are my grandparents, Eugenie and Saly Goldstein. Between them is Uncle Lother.

My father was discharged from the German army in 1918 and eventually started working at a company that manufactured personal consumer items made of rubber, such as prophylactics and little shields for under the arm, which women used to protect their clothing from perspiration. The company was in Berlin and owned by a man named Jakob Grubner.

The Grubner family was of strictly Jewish-Polish stock. They had probably immigrated to Germany in the 1800s in pursuit of a better life. They were observant Jews and lived according to the rules and customs of the religion. Thus it was a bit of an oddity that Jakob's sister, Rita, had not married, since religious families expected their daughters to marry young. Rita, however, was stubborn. She stood only 4 feet 10 inches tall, but her stature belied her zest: she had gone on her own to study in France, smoked cigarettes before it was fashionable for women to do so, dressed like a flapper, and fixed her hair so that she was always on trend. The worldly and stylish Rita also worked as a traveling saleswoman. She had had her share of suitors, being from a commercially successful family and a Paris-educated university graduate, and she wanted a man who would be her equal.

Their parents had died relatively young, so it fell to Jakob to find a husband for Rita. In a last-gasp effort, Jakob took a chance and introduced Hermann to Rita. And love being what it is, Rita proved to be the right match for the dashing Hermann. They married in 1927. My mother was 35 years old; my father, 31.

Rita Goldstein, my mother

Hermann Goldstein, my father

Pamela Sampson

My parents subsequently set up household in a spacious apartment on Clausewitzstrasse, very close to the Kurfurstendamm, a bustling, fashionable commercial boulevard in the heart of Berlin that was often compared to the Champs-Élysées in Paris. I was born just a year later, on October 30, 1928. My name wasn't Henry back then; it was Heinz.

My father began a new career selling cosmetics for a wholesaler whose name was Mr. Mautner. Then, after acquiring some experience, my father joined forces with a former chemist, and they manufactured their own perfume. One room in our spacious apartment was dedicated as a laboratory for creating the perfume, and its flowery scent was ever-present in our home. My father would take these perfumes, as well as soaps, colognes and other items, to sell at barbers and salons around Berlin.

My mother had a separate business. She would buy sterling silver items, like trays and serving pieces, from factories and resell them to clients for wedding gifts and other occasions. So our six-room apartment was a busy place, like a luxury emporium, with lots of pleasant noises and smells and my parents enthusiasm for entrepreneurship forging their bond.

My mother insisted on keeping certain Jewish rituals, such as observing the weekly Sabbath by lighting candles and saying prayers and by keeping a kosher kitchen. My father didn't really care one way or the other, and he went along with my mother to keep her happy.

NO REPLY

These were not necessarily easy times. Like the entire industrialized West, Germany in the early 1930s was reeling from the effects of an economic crash: unemployment was extremely high; banks had collapsed and people had lost their savings.

But those years for me were the only trouble-free years of my life. My parents had created for us a small bubble of joy. Little did we know how short-lived our happiness would be.

CHAPTER 2

FOR ME, LIKE all Jews in Europe, life as we knew it began its spiral into violent collapse on January 30, 1933. That was the day Hitler became chancellor of Germany, and it wasn't long before persecution of his opponents began.

I started school at age 6, about a year after Hitler came to power. My parents sent me off with a large, cornucopia-shaped cone full of candy, little gifts and school supplies. It was a longstanding German tradition for a child to be given a Schultuete on the first day of school to help ease any anxieties.

I entered the Judische Volksschule Fasanenstrasse in the Charlottenburg borough of Berlin. It was a Jewish school held inside the Fasanenstrasse Synagogue, a magnificent structure built in 1912, with large domes, marble columns and grand, sculpted lions at the entrance portal. Emperor Wilhelm II is said to have visited the temple upon its opening, such was its grandeur. We lived very close to this beautiful synagogue, and I remember walking there for school.

I didn't notice much anti-Semitism just after Hitler assumed power. My friends were both Jewish and Christian.

NO REPLY

We were friendly with the family of the building superintendent, who was a Christian, and he would invite me to his apartment on Christmas to see the lights on his tree.

When my father paid sales calls, he occasionally brought me along. His clients were Jews and non-Jews, and I never noticed a difference between them. My father got along with everyone. For lunch, we would stop at restaurants and order rabbit stew. This traditional German stew is made from rabbit and a marinade of wine and vinegar. My father was especially fond of this dish, even though rabbit meat is strictly out of bounds for those who keep kosher. My father and I of course did this on the sly; my mother would have been aghast. Yet these are among my best memories, going in hand with my father around Berlin, stopping in shops to make sales and then rewarding ourselves at a restaurant with a rabbit stew dinner.

This innocent pleasure soon became off-limits as the Nazis implemented their plans to segregate Jews from society and strip them of their rights. Signs sprang up on all sorts of establishments barring Jews from entering. I remember one sign in particular: "Dogs and Jews not wanted." We were no longer allowed in restaurants.

There was a tree-lined park near our apartment where I used to play. One day, I noticed that the benches had been painted; some were green and some were yellow. Signs appeared that said Jews were not allowed to sit on the green benches, only the yellow ones. Jews were eventually banned from a host of public areas like cinemas, theaters, cafés, parks, swimming pools and libraries.

Pamela Sampson

Among the first of the 400 decrees aimed at removing Jews from daily life was enacted just weeks after Hitler assumed power: it demanded that Jews be fired from positions in the civil service, causing many to lose jobs and thus their income. It was the first step toward impoverishing the Jews, which would make it very difficult to leave later on.

The law even applied to Jewish veterans who had fought for Germany in World War I. Some 100,000 Jews had been enlisted in the German Imperial Army; they had shared the same deprivations on the battlefield as the Christians, and their deaths were just as final. But their sacrifices counted for nothing under Hitler.

There were many stories of Hitler Youth waiting outside Jewish schools to beat up children. Fortunately I didn't experience that, but I remember a humiliating moment involving a Christian boy who had been my friend. I was showing a Mont Blanc ballpoint pen that my parents had given me for my birthday to a group of friends when this boy grabbed the pen from me and wrote "JUDE" on my forehead.

The one person in my family who sensed the danger early on was my Uncle Walter, a younger brother of my father. Shortly after Hitler came to power, Walter decided to leave Germany for Palestine. Walter had been an editor for the *Berliner Tageblatt*, the most widely read German newspaper at the time. Unlike many Jews who believed that Hitler was a passing fancy, Walter was convinced Hitler was dangerous and was there to stay.

What may also have contributed to Walter's decision to emigrate was passage of a law in October 1933 called

10

the Editor's Law. This law forbade Jews and those married to Jews from working in journalism. Newspapers were placed under Nazi control, and it became impossible for Jewish journalists to work.

Jewish children were being kicked out of schools because of quotas limiting their numbers. Any Jew who stayed faced harassment by non-Jewish students and especially by teachers. Looking for a safe haven for me, my parents settled on a boarding school for Jewish children in the countryside. It was outside of Potsdam, in the same village where Albert Einstein had had a summer home, and was called Landschulheim Caputh.

The school had originally opened as a holiday camp for Jewish children but expanded into a bona fide school because of the need for schooling for Jewish children. There were excursions, games, musical evenings and swimming at the lake. My parents thought I would be safer in the countryside.

But there really was no place to be safe under Hitler. On the morning of November 9, 1938, I was playing on the Caputh soccer field when suddenly dozens of Hitler Youth appeared. They ran amok on the field, broke into the dormitory, grabbed chairs and tables and started throwing them out the windows. They threw out the bedding and beds. They entered the kitchen, grabbed food that was cooking on the stoves and poured everything onto the floor. They swore at us, calling us Jewish bastards.

"You really think we weren't going to come get you?" one of them shouted at me. I was 10 years old.

Pamela Sampson

I was so terrified by this attack that I seem to have blocked out my memories of how I escaped. To this day, I have no recollection of how I made it back to my parents' apartment in Berlin. However, another student at Caputh who was interviewed years later said that taxis had been ordered for the smaller children, as well as those who were ill, who could not walk to Potsdam. The other children split up into small groups in order to go unnoticed, and walked through the woods to the train station at Potsdam. The children were told not to walk along the road; a Jew appearing in public was risking his or her life.

What I do remember is the shock I felt when I returned to Berlin and saw what was happening. The beloved Fasanenstrasse Synagogue where I had gone to school was on fire. Flames rose from the pews to the cupolas; black smoke poured out the windows.

Firefighters were on the scene but had received prior orders not to put the fire out. They had been stationed near synagogues throughout Germany to make sure that buildings adjacent to synagogues, those owned by Christians, did not catch fire.

This was the infamous Kristallnacht, commonly known as the "Night of Broken Glass," a full-blown anti-Jewish pogrom that took place in Germany and Austria on November 9-10, 1938. Mobs of stormtroopers and Hitler Youth roamed the streets with clubs, sledgehammers and other weapons, destroying Jewish-owned shops, homes and synagogues and leaving a frothing sea of shattered glass and human blood in their wake.

NO REPLY

Jewish men were arrested randomly, picked right off the street. There was a lot of panic and nowhere to turn for help. Almost 300 synagogues — nearly every synagogue in Germany — were burned down. Men between the ages of 16 and 60 were arrested at home and on the street. Everyone was trying to hide. My father managed to escape arrest by riding the subway all night.

Then the Jews were punished for Kristallnacht, an early show of the sadism that Nazis delighted in. Owners of the more than 7,000 destroyed stores were forced to clean up the streets, and the Jewish community was fined for the damage. On November 12, 1938, the German government decreed that Jews should pay an "atonement fine" of one billion German marks. On the same day, all Jewish-owned retail stores were ordered closed. The next month, the squeeze intensified: the German government announced its intention to liquidate all real estate, companies, and securities owned by Jews.

At this point, Germany's notorious concentration camp system was in its early stages. Three concentration camps — Dachau, Sachsenhausen, and Buchenwald — were in operation at this time, mostly for political opponents of the regime. These camps were where the Jewish men who were arrested during Kristallnacht were sent.

I remember walking along the Kurfurstendamm and seeing the glass on the sidewalk — piles and piles of shards; stores completely destroyed; inventories from shops dumped out of the stores. Perhaps half the stores on the entire boulevard were damaged or destroyed. It hadn't been clear to me until this moment just how many stores were Jewish-owned. The Nazis knew which businesses were Jewish and were careful to avoid breaking the windows of stores owned by Christians.

I remember one store called Geiger, where they sold yarn for knitting. The Nazis weren't sure whether this store was Jewish- or Christian-owned, so a big question mark had been painted on the front. After an investigation was made, the windows were shattered.

By the time Kristallnacht was over, nearly 100 Jews were dead and 30,000 had been arrested and placed in camps. My parents were lucky insofar as they did not operate a store; they conducted their businesses out of our apartment and eluded the rampage. But Kristallnacht was a turning point for my parents; they realized the Nazis were bent on destroying the Jewish community and that escaping Germany was a matter of life and death.

My parents sold every possession that they could to raise money to leave the country. On February 21, 1939, the Nazis issued a decree ordering Jews to turn over all of their gold and silver. I don't know if my mother liquidated her business before this decree. If not, her inventory would have been confiscated right then and there, without any compensation.

Thousands of Jews desperately seeking visas out of Germany could be seen lining up at foreign consulates. My parents were among them. We had obtained a quota number that placed us on a waiting list for visas for the

United States. But the U.S. was not giving out many visas, and the waiting list was extremely long. We couldn't wait.

The Fasanenstrasse Synagogue in Berlin engulfed in flames during Kristallnacht, November 9, 1938. (Courtesy of The Associated Press)

CHAPTER 3

It was announced in April 1939 that the luxury ocean liner MS St. Louis would make a special voyage from Hamburg to Havana the next month; tickets sold out immediately. My parents were among more than 900 people lucky enough to obtain passage for this trip. We also had to buy Cuban landing certificates so we could stay in Cuba while waiting for our visas to enter the United States.

The U.S. was only just pulling out of the Great Depression, the worst economic crisis in its history, and was not anxious to accept refugees. Anxiety about unemployment was very high, and new workers from abroad were not wanted. Xenophobia, fear of Communist and other so-called subversive elements, and anti-Semitism were the rule, rather than the exception. A poll published by Fortune Magazine in 1938 showed 83 percent of respondents opposed relaxing immigration quotas. Other polls consistently showed firm opposition among the American people for allowing more European refugees into the country. The opposition even extended to children.

So strict immigration restrictions were in place, reflecting popular will. To obtain a visa to enter the country, an applicant had to have five copies of the visa application; two copies of the birth certificate; a quota number establishing the applicant's place on the waiting list for a visa; two U.S. citizens as sponsors who had to provide tax returns, bank account information, an affidavit from an employer or other responsible party, and six notarized copies of a statement of financial support and sponsorship; a certificate of good conduct from German police, including two copies of police, military and any other government records; and a physical examination at a U.S. consulate.

In addition, starting September 30, 1939, applicants had to have proof of permission to leave Germany and proof of booked passage to a Western hemisphere destination. In September 1940, affidavits of good conduct from responsible, disinterested parties were also required. This oppressive process only slowed down what was the last chance of escape for many German Jews.

U.S. immigration law limited the number of immigrants to roughly 154,000 a year and eligibility was determined by where you came from. This law, somewhat racist in nature, favored foreigners planning to settle permanently in the U.S. from places like Britain and the Nordic countries and was designed to keep out Jews, Italians and others who might disturb America's "ethnic balance."

While the year 1939 marked the first time that the United States actually let in the maximum number of people allowed under its quota, it hardly met the need. Some 27,000 spaces were available, but 309,000 Jews from Germany, Austria and the annexed territory of Czechoslovakia had applied — my family among them. Our quota number wasn't high enough to get into the U.S. in 1939.

Meanwhile, the cost of the Cuban landing certificates was very high. We had paid, I believe, about $480 for three of them. That would be the equivalent of about $8,000 today. The ship tickets were also expensive; the Nazis of course made everyone buy round-trip tickets even though no one planned to return to Germany.

We were lucky to still have financial resources in 1938, because Hitler had been on a steady campaign to break the Jews from the moment he came to power. Between 1933 and 1939, laws and decrees were passed left and right to degrade Jews and isolate them from the rest of society. Jewish officers were expelled from the army; Jewish lawyers lost their licenses to practice; Jewish doctors were banned from treating non-Jewish patients; Jewish students were kicked out of public schools and universities. Virtually all Jewish-owned property was seized. On top of it all, Germany levied a 25 percent "flight tax" on any substantial property or income on any Jew applying to emigrate.

These measures had devastating financial consequences on the community. Many Jews had been thrust into absolute poverty, making it impossible to get out. We felt very lucky that my uncle had done well in his rubber manufacturing business, and the family still had resources to pay for the tickets and immigration documents.

St. Louis passengers were only allowed to take 10 German marks onto the ship, or about $4 each. In lieu of money, my father put items from his perfume business into a luggage case in hopes of resuming work as soon as we landed in Cuba.

Boarding the St. Louis was an adventure for me. I had never in my life seen anything as immense or as beautiful as this eight-deck, 16,732-ton ship, with its graceful staircases and glittering chandeliers. The vessel belonged to the Hamburg-Amerika line, known as Hapag, a shipping line that had been Germany's pride and joy on the high seas thanks to a young Jewish shipping magnate named Albert Ballin. He became director of the line in 1888, at a time when it was hammered by competition and bad management, and built it into the world's largest shipping line. But after Hitler assumed power, the company fell under Nazi control. Now, ironically, one of its ships, flying the swastika flag, was being used to move unwanted Jews out of Germany.

Pamela Sampson

We set sail on May 13, 1939. To be honest, I don't remember feeling deep sorrow. I was 10 years old, and I had my parents. That was what mattered to me. Kristallnacht, and the terror I had experienced and witnessed, had made me understand that our lives were in danger in Germany. I accepted that it was necessary to go to Cuba, where we would wait until we got our visas for America.

A view of the MS St. Louis surrounded by smaller vessels in the port of Hamburg (Courtesy of the United States Holocaust Memorial Museum)

I know the adults had a much harder time saying good-bye; there were tears. Most had been born in

Germany and held it to be the most enlightened of civilizations. The adults on board were stupefied by the brutal ejection from a homeland where their families had been born and buried for generations.

My mother's sister, Berta, and her family had escaped Germany just two weeks before we did. They arrived in Cuba on a ship called the "Iberia" with about 250 other passengers and were waiting for us in Havana. In fact, there were several thousand Jewish refugees in Havana by the time we bought our tickets. It made things easier on my parents, knowing that we already had family in Cuba.

As the St. Louis plied through the rough Atlantic, the biting winds and glorious purity of the open seas helped calm our anxieties. Passengers reclined on deck chairs under wool blankets in the restorative sunshine. As Germany faded from view, people's nerves eased. There were parties and balloons. There was a cinema. A swing band played for couples to dance in the ballroom. There was even a small swimming pool on deck. The boys played pretty roughly; I struggled to get out of the pool after someone jumped on top of me. I nearly died right then and there.

We also played games in the lifeboats and pulled assorted pranks. I heard that some mischievous kids soaped the door handles to the bathrooms. But not me!

A celebration on board the St. Louis. I am seated
in the center, facing the camera. (Courtesy of the
United States Holocaust Memorial Museum)

My parents (seated at the right) on board the MS St. Louis.
Their happy times were soon to end forever. (Courtesy
of the United States Holocaust Memorial Museum)

NO REPLY

I remember there was a large picture of Hitler in the big dining room but it was either taken down for Friday night Sabbath services or covered with a cloth. I don't remember exactly how they hid the portrait of Hitler — but I do know that we weren't forced to look at him while we prayed.

In retrospect, it is quite stunning to think of how bold the ship's captain, Gustav Schroeder, was in ordering Hitler's portrait out of view. Schroeder was, in fact, an anti-Nazi and very sympathetic to our plight. His goal was to ensure us a courteous, comfortable trip. But after five years of harassment, discrimination and abuse at the hands of the Nazis, many passengers just could not relax.

The trip from Hamburg to Havana took about two weeks. I remember almost to the minute the moment when the ship reached the Cuban shoreline on May 27. We were awakened by a loud horn before dawn for an early breakfast. Everyone was excited. We brought our suitcases onto the deck. My first impression was of the air: tropical, humid, and totally different from Germany. Visions of rum, cigars and sun-washed shores dazzled everyone. We could see native Cubans diving for coins in the harbor's shallow waters and fruit sellers stocking pineapples in their boats. But hours passed. It became blistering hot on deck as we stood, waiting for permission to walk down the gangplank and onto land.

What we didn't know was that our Cuban landing certificates were worthless. The certificates had been issued and personally signed by Cuban immigration director-general Manuel Benitez Gonzalez, and we had no reason to suspect they were not valid. But Gonzalez was a notorious profiteer: he had amassed a fortune by using his position to issue overpriced travel documents to unsuspecting refugees. In our case, the documents had been invalidated a week before we left Germany.

That was because Gonzalez had rivals within the Cuban government, including President Federico Laredo Bru, who it seemed had finally gotten fed up with Gonzalez's notorious moneymaking scheme and decided to shut it down. On May 5, a week before the St. Louis departed Germany, the Cuban government declared Gonzalez's landing certificates null and void. From that point on, immigrants would have to obtain written authorization from the Cuban secretaries of state and labor and post a $500 bond in advance of entry into Cuba.

So the permits were invalidated just days before we sailed, and we didn't know it. The Nazis knew, of course, and yet they allowed us to sail. That is why they required us to pay for return passage to Germany. They also wanted to use the St. Louis for propaganda. They wanted the world to see that Germany was allowing Jews to leave, but that no one wanted us.

Much to our shock, we weren't allowed off the ship. My Aunt Berta, my Uncle Willy and my cousin Manfred rented a boat and rowed up to the St. Louis. Many other relatives who were already in Cuba did the same. Soon the St. Louis was surrounded by little vessels full of relatives of passengers delivering words of love and encouragement: "Don't give up!" they shouted.

The St. Louis was ordered not to dock; it was forced to drop anchor in the middle of the harbor.

Meanwhile, Captain Schroeder had received a cable from Hapag's home office in Germany on May 23, saying that the St. Louis passengers were holding invalid permits and might not be able to disembark. Schroeder understood this meant trouble and immediately convened a small committee of passengers, confiding in them the possibility that Cuba might not let us in.

The passenger committee sent an urgent cable to the Jewish Joint Relief Committee in Havana, which immediately notified its head office in New York: the American Jewish Joint Distribution Committee, the largest Jewish aid agency in the world.

The Joint urgently dispatched to Cuba two people, attorney Lawrence Berenson and Cecilia Razovsky, on May 29 to try to help us. Berenson had been president of the Cuban-American Chamber of Commerce, spoke fluent Spanish, and was seen as the best person to negotiate on behalf of the passengers. Razovsky was there to assist. But they faced serious roadblocks: corruption in Cuba, an unwillingness of the U.S. to force Havana's hand, and agitation by fascist forces at work on the Caribbean island. We were being squeezed from many sides.

Pamela Sampson

The Cuban Nazi Party was granted official status just seven months before we landed, and it had been working hard to stir up anti-Semitism among the local population. Cuban newspapers owned by right-wing families printed inflammatory articles against Jews. The *Diario de la Marina* wrote in early May that a thousand Jews would be headed for Cuba in mid-May "and once they land they look for and obtain work, displacing Cuban workers."

Labor unions also had been agitating against us. Bru was very sensitive to worker and union sentiment; their power had been expanded under his watch, and he would need their support in any upcoming election. Additionally, two other ships carrying Jewish refugees had arrived in Cuba within 24 hours of the St. Louis, adding to rumors that Communist-sympathizing Jews were inundating the island and threatening to take jobs away.

The U.S. government, which didn't want a disturbance of its Good Neighbor Policy with Latin America, officially indicated it would not intervene. However, American diplomats in Cuba, including Ambassador J. Butler Wright and Consul General Coert du Bois, tried informally to nudge the Cubans toward a humanitarian solution and maintained behind-the-scenes contact with both Berenson and high-level Cuban officials.

Frantic negotiations began on June 1, when Berenson met with Bru. The Cuban president took the position that he would not negotiate while the St. Louis was still in Cuba's territorial waters. So on June 2, after a week in the blinding sun, the St. Louis raised anchor and left. By this time, the St. Louis was front-page news across the United States. Tensions were extremely high; one passenger cut his wrists and threw himself overboard, trying to kill himself. He was fished out of the harbor and brought to a hospital in Cuba, but his family was not allowed to join him.

Captain Schroeder sailed the ship toward Florida, hoping the United States would allow us in. Schroeder could have steered the ship straight back to Germany, but he recognized the danger we were in. Undaunted, he did everything in his power to find us safe harbor.

Nearly everyone on board ultimately dreamed of going to America, a land renown for freedom and opportunity for all who entered. Messages, letters and postcards flooded into the State Department in support of us.

But tragically, America had more pressing concerns than us 900 refugees.

As mentioned, anti-immigrant sentiment in America was very high. The U.S. State Department refused to take any steps to allow the St. Louis passengers in. The chief of the visa division, A.M. Warren, issued a decision that the refugees on board the St. Louis "must await their turns on the waiting list and then qualify for and obtain immigration visas" before they could enter the United States.

On June 3, Berenson submitted an offer to Bru's negotiating team, which included a $50,000 bond guaranteeing that the passengers would not become dependent on Cuba for financial assistance. Bru made a counterproposal, raising the bond to $150,000 and some other stipulations. However, the next day, Berenson was stunned to learn that Bru's offer was in addition to a $500 cash bond for each passenger, meaning another $450,000 had to be raised.

The money was promised to Bru the next day, June 5. Bru announced that a 48-hour deadline had been set for negotiations to be completed.

But events overtook Berenson, who apparently had thought — and was gravely mistaken by doing so — that there was room for back-and-forth bargaining and that he could possibly drive the price down. On June 6, newspapers reported a statement by Cuban Secretary of the Treasury Joaquin Ochotorena to the effect that Bru's conditions for the landing of the St. Louis passengers had not been met and that they would not be permitted to enter Cuba.

So all the intense negotiations were to no avail, even though the Joint had agreed to meet any financial demand. Berenson miscalculated his ability to intervene. He had connections in Cuba but not the right ones. (Berenson was an intimate of Cuban strongman Colonel Fulgencio Batista, who was a clear foe of Bru).

Colonel Fulgencio Batista and Lawrence Berenson
with their wives in New York in November 1938.
(Courtesy of The Associated Press)

Bru had appeared to waiver, making some initial ges-
tures that hinted at compromise. But in the end, he dug
in his heels: this was an internal political battle that he
wanted to win. Bru ordered the ship out of Cuban waters.

Desperate for help, the passenger committee sent an
urgent wireless message to President Roosevelt. "Help
them, Mr. President, the 900 passengers, of which more
than 400 are women and children."

There was no reply. With public sentiment against immigrants, Roosevelt was not willing to run political risks for us.

The ordeal of the St. Louis had by now come to the attention of Canada, where a small group of influential citizens lobbied the government to help. But the plea was in vain. The Canadian government refused to help. Immigration director Frederick Blair would go down somewhat infamously in history for proclaiming that no country "could open its doors wide enough to take in the hundreds of thousands of Jewish people who want to leave Europe: the line must be drawn somewhere."

The St. Louis shifted course and began to head back to Europe.

Captain Schroeder maintained the ship at the slowest speed possible in order to buy time. One passenger had already attempted suicide, and Schroeder was afraid that many more would do the same. He even considered deliberately shipwrecking the St. Louis off the coast of England in order to force the British to take us in.

There was panic on board. Meetings were held instead of festivities, and progress in negotiations was relayed to the passengers. Rumors abounded about where we might or might not be headed.

The Joint set to work trying to find countries that would accept us passengers. Emergency cables went out to the heads of governments in Britain, France and elsewhere, desperately pleading for a place to land.

Critically, the Joint agreed to provide financial guarantees of support to any country willing to take in the passengers. This guarantee for support led to a break-through in Britain.

Paul Baerwald, the head of the Joint, was in London at the time, working with the Intergovernmental Committee on Refugees. In a communication to Robert Pell, a U.S. State Department official working at the ICR, Baerwald relayed that the Joint had pledged "financial support guarantees" to any country willing to take the St. Louis passengers.

On continental Europe, Morris Troper, the Joint's head in Paris, worked closely with Max Gottschalk, head of the Belgian Refugee Committee in Brussels, and managed to win a pledge from Belgium on Saturday, June 10: Prime Minister Hubert Pierlot and King Leopold III agreed to accept 200 passengers.

Two days later, Troper received word that Holland's Queen Wilhelmina and the Dutch government had agreed to temporarily take in refugees. Finally, by mid-June, places for all the passengers had been secured in four European countries: Great Britain would take 288 refugees; Belgium, 214; France, 224; and the Netherlands, 181.

There was some effort to allow families to choose the country where they would go. My parents requested France because my father was in the perfume business, and he thought he might have a chance at establishing himself there. In addition, my mother had studied in Paris and spoke French.

Passengers also completed questionnaires that asked for names of friends and relatives in the four countries offering refuge and the status of their applications for American visas. The refugees were being granted only temporary asylum and had to agree to eventually leave the country offering asylum to permanent homes elsewhere.

On June 17, more than a month after the St. Louis had left Hamburg, the vessel neared the Dutch port of Flushing. There, a tugboat brought the Joint's Morris Troper up to the ship, and he boarded. Eleven-year-old Liesl Joseph read a letter of thanks from all of the children. He and others had saved our lives.

The St. Louis docked in Antwerp, Belgium, later that day. From there, the families divided up and said good-bye.

We left the St. Louis and boarded the Rhakotis, a freighter that would drop passengers off in France and Britain. My mother, father and I arrived in Boulogne, France, on June 20, 1939. We thought we were safe — but the next year, German troops would march into Paris.

CHAPTER 4

FRANCE WAS NOT an easy place for strangers in the 1930s. Foreign workers had been welcomed after World War I, but this was no longer the case by the time we sought refuge there. The fact was that France was inundated with refugees from the west and east.

To the west was Spain, where a bloody civil war had been raging, causing hundreds of thousands of Spanish refugees and anti-Franco fighters to flee. By the spring of 1939, more than 450,000 Spanish refugees had reached France. The country was ill-equipped to handle the mass inpouring and hastily set up scores of internment camps.

To the east, meanwhile, Jews and other opponents of Hitler in Germany and Austria were rushing into France to escape persecution. This came at a time in France of political and economic instability, and the influx was not exactly welcomed.

Thus when the St. Louis landed in France, we weren't free to go where we wanted. The families were separated: the men from the women, the children from the adults.

Families were forced apart, sent in all directions without much thought; war was looming.

I had to say good-bye to both my parents, but I don't remember the exact moment. I was being handed over to complete strangers in a strange country. No one had anticipated this. We thought we were headed into safe hands when we first boarded the St. Louis, but now we were back in Europe, where Hitler's army was metastasizing like an aggressive cancer.

The Jewish community in France had a rescue network aimed at saving children called Oeuvre de Secours aux Enfants (the Society for the Rescue of Children), or OSE. This group was founded in Russia in 1912 by a group of Jewish doctors who wanted to help impoverished and ill children. It moved its headquarters to Berlin in 1923 and then to France in 1933 as the Nazis came to power.

The OSE, which later became an active part of the French Resistance, was managing large homes for Jewish children, many of German origin, whose parents had been arrested or deported. More than 200 children had found shelter in OSE homes by the spring of 1939, and I joined them in June of that year. I was sent to a place called Villa Helvetia, which was located in Montmorency, just north of Paris.

Loneliness overwhelmed me. Even when we were forced to leave Germany, my mother and father were by my side. But now, I was disoriented, being separated

NO REPLY

from my parents. The next few months would be full of longing for my "Mutti" and "Papi."

My parents were also separated from each other. My mother was sent to Le Mans, a city southwest of Paris, and housed in a small room in a little hotel. These small 'pensions' were empty of tourists but packed with refugees. A lot of people from the St. Louis went to Le Mans.

My father faced an entirely different fate. France at that time considered Germany a hostile country, and my father was considered an enemy alien. It didn't matter that he was Jewish and a victim of Hitler's persecution. Very shortly after his arrival in France, he was put into an internment camp.

We had been in France just a few months when Hitler launched his lightning war against Poland on September 1, 1939; the German army rapidly smashed through Polish defenses. Britain and France, which had a pact with Poland, declared war on Germany a few days later. It was the start of World War II.

But I was a little boy — and, truthfully, accustomed to being spoiled and doted upon as an only child — and my thoughts centered on my loneliness. I was miserable at Villa Helvetia without my parents. It was also terribly frightening. We had gas masks, in case the Germans decided to fight with poison gas, as they did in World War I.

Germany's attack on Western Europe began in May 1940.

VILLA HELVETIA. — *Maison de Repinire*, Rue des Carrières, Montmorency (S.-et-O.). Téléph. 31-11

Villa Helvetia in Montmorency, France. (Courtesy of
the United States Holocaust Memorial Museum)

It had taken only a few weeks for the French army to
be completely routed. It was a total shock: the Germans
invaded through Belgium and avoided the strongest
fortifications along the Maginot Line that were built
specifically as a military buffer to keep France safe
from a German invasion. The French government fled
Paris on June 10. Two days later, in order to prevent the
Wehrmacht from destroying Paris, the government declared it an "open city," meaning no efforts to defend it
would be taken.

The Germans entered Paris on June 14, and
two days later French Prime Minister Paul Reynaud

resigned. The French army capitulated and an armistice was signed between France and Germany on June 22. Hitler toured Paris the next day. Now every St. Louis passenger who had found refuge in France was in mortal danger.

We received no official information on the whereabouts of my father. We were able to trace him only via letters that he was permitted to send. I believe he was initially placed in a camp in Fresnay-sur-Sarthe and then transferred to a larger camp called St. Cyprien.

Located just a few miles from the border with Spain, the St. Cyprien internment camp was hastily built in February 1939 to house Spanish refugees. Some 90,000 of them had been interned there before my father arrived.

Then it became a place to detain Jewish refugees.

Soon, thousands of Jews were incarcerated there, basically under arrest. The initial intention was just to house all these refugees somewhere — but once France and Germany had an armistice, the Jews in the camps were no longer refugees. They were hostages.

I was able to visit my father once or twice while he was being held in a camp and remember seeing him behind barbed wire. This was very, very painful.

Many documents have been uncovered after the war, as well as accounts from survivors, that describe how terrible conditions were at St. Cyprien and just about all the other internment camps. It shocks the intellect to acknowledge that an enlightened country like France would allow so many innocent people to languish of near-starvation, neglect and disease.

A report by a caseworker from the Joint who visited St. Cyprien in July 1940 underscored the inhumane treatment that the refugees endured. The report described the camp as completely primitive and lacking in every necessity. There was no electricity or running water. It was surrounded by long rows of barbed wire; its barracks were made of planks and corrugated iron. The floors were simply dirt. There was no furniture, no medical care, no sanitation whatsoever.

In the summer of 1940, internees registered a strong protest with the Committee Internationale de Croix Rouge (International Committee of the Red Cross). They complained of contaminated water, unbearable flies, mice, rats, lice and straw mattresses infested with vermin; defective housing; and a lack of food, clothing, hygiene and medical care. By August 1940, 85 percent of internees had dysentery. A typhoid epidemic around that time killed 17 people in three weeks.

That same summer, an ominous sign emerged of France's collaboration with the enemy: a law forbidding anti-Semitism in the media was repealed. That meant it was no longer illegal to print material that disparaged and humiliated Jews. The stage was being set for the destruction of the Jews in France.

NO REPLY

Because I was so unhappy at Villa Helvetia, my mother brought me to Le Mans. I have several vivid memories of being there: one, of sleeping on top of a suitcase, since I had no bed; and two, of British soldiers leaving the area during the prolonged evacuation of Dunkirk: the headquarters of the southern portion of the British Expeditionary Force had been at Chateau de la Blanchardiere in Le Mans.

My mother decided to leave Le Mans in an effort to improve our living circumstances. She made contact with a cousin, Siegfried Schnelling, who lived in Paris. He was a goldsmith whose specialty was designing circular frames for collectors' coins to protect them from damage. The frames were expertly crafted; the renowned Tiffany Co. carried them. Uncle Siegfried had moved to France in the 1930s while Germany was still allowing Jews to leave, and he paid for us to stay in a small room at the Hotel du Conservatoire on rue de l'Echiquier (Echiquier Street) in Paris' 10th arrondissement near Bonne Nouvelle metro station.

We were in Paris when the Germans marched in. I remember the fear and astonishment on the faces of the French.

Under the armistice, France was effectively divided into two zones. The northern zone, or occupied zone that included Paris, was controlled by Germany. The southern, so-called free zone was quasi-independent and had its headquarters in the small town of Vichy.

The head of government was Pétain, the World War I military hero.

At first, we didn't have a very difficult time under the occupation. My mother, who spoke fluent French, and I had been in France for a year by that time and were able to get around with ease. To make some pocket money, I took German officers shopping to the big department stores, where they bought stockings and perfume for their wives and girlfriends. These occupiers had plenty of money — likely much of it stolen from those occupied — and they gave me big tips for helping them around. In that regard, I was sort of an unsuspecting collaborator.

These soldiers were not immensely political and didn't seem to care about why my mother and I were in Paris; it's very possible that they knew we were Jews. Not every German fell prey to Hitler's idiotic ranting about Jews, at least not during the initial phase of the war.

There were no SS that I remember in Paris at the time, just Wehrmacht officers. These soldiers were from small towns, where cordial relations between Jew and German had been the rule rather than the exception. I clearly remember on numerous occasions being seated at a café with my mother and four or five German soldiers. As strange as it seems, my mother and I would meet German soldiers around Paris and share cake and coffee with them.

NO REPLY

Soon the good times came to an end, and radically so. In October 1940, the Vichy government issued a law that banned Jews from many professions: the civil service, the officer corps, teaching, journalism, theater, radio and cinema. This step toward disenfranchising and impoverishing Jews made them much easier targets. That same month, a law was passed aimed at foreign Jews like us. It gave prefects, or local government administrators, the power to arrest Jews from Germany, Austria and other countries and intern them in camps.

Blanket arrests of Jews began in France in 1940 and rose in 1941. Jewish male adults who were not French citizens were ordered to appear before the police. There, they were placed under immediate arrest and then sent to internment camps. France also began confiscating Jewish property and businesses. The noose was tightening.

My mother keenly felt the danger living under German occupation and decided we had to leave. We headed for the unoccupied zone in August 1941 and ended up in Nice. Somehow we managed to cross the demarcation line between the two zones, although I don't remember the trip or whether we went by train or some other way. Luckily, my mother was very resourceful; soon we had a safe place to stay in Nice, a small hotel called the Hotel Rambaldi on Boulevard Rambaldi. It had a bed, a tiny closet, a table and two chairs.

My father, meanwhile, was hundreds of miles away, near the Spanish border in an internment camp called Gurs. This camp, one of the largest, was originally established to hold Spanish Republican soldiers after their defeat in Spain's Civil War. Like other camps, Gurs was overcrowded, and filthy. There was little food, little water, no sanitation and no medical care. Hundreds of detainees died of typhoid fever, dysentery and other diseases in 1940-41.

Meanwhile, I turned 13 years old on October 30, 1941; it was time for my bar mitzvah, a special religious rite of passage for Jewish males. We had been on the run since May 1939. I had missed more than two years of school and bar mitzvah lessons. But we were in fact extremely fortunate to celebrate this event in Nice, for in that month, seven synagogues in Paris had been bombed.

My mother was determined that I should have my bar mitzvah as usual, despite the circumstances and the increasingly dangerous atmosphere. More than anything else, she wanted my father to attend. In order to try to secure his temporary release from Gurs, she wrote a letter to the local government official of the region of Pau, where Gurs was located.

In a letter dated September 9, 1941, my mother wrote: "I have the honor of soliciting your kindness in requesting a leave of absence for several weeks for my husband, Hermann Goldstein, to attend the communion of our only child ... We belong to the group of passengers from the St. Louis ship which received asylum in France ... I dare to hope, Monsieur, that you will grant us the favor of permitting my husband to attend the celebration of his son, whom he hasn't seen for more than two years." She even offered to put up a bond of 25,000 francs to guarantee my father's return.

But we received no reply. Until her death, my mother swore never to forgive France.

My father also tried to get out with the help of a certain Dr. Ansbacher, who it appears was a German rabbi interned at Gurs but who seemed to have contacts beyond the barbed wire, according historical records. We waited and waited for a response.

My father, sensing that the appeals might be ignored or rejected, wrote me a letter, addressed to his "beloved little Heinz," on November 3, 1941:

"Accept my dearest child, my most heart-felt wishes, and I will on this day of honor pray to God that he will protect you all of your life ... Strive to be a meaningful member of human society and distinguish yourself with honesty, a sense of duty so that you deserve the esteem of those around you. ... Even though I cannot be with you and your dearest mother, in spirit I am with you. And on Shabbat I will pray to God that when you read the portion of the Torah, that I am thinking of you, and I will imagine in my mind that I hear your beautiful voice."

Pamela Sampson

The letter that I wrote to my father after it became apparent he would not be attending my bar mitzvah.

44

NO REPLY

Thus the bar mitzvah took place without my father. It was held in an apartment that was also used as a place of worship, and I remember the rabbi trying to console me because my father wasn't there.

Each week, a portion of the Jewish Bible, or Torah, is read in synagogue. The Torah portion that was due to be read at the time of my bar mitzvah is called Akedei Itzhak — the Binding of Isaac. In this famed story, God commands Abraham to offer his son, Isaac, as a sacrifice. After Isaac is bound to an altar and Abraham prepares to kill him, the angel of God stops Abraham at the last minute, saying, "now I know you fear God." At that point, Abraham sees a ram in some nearby bushes and sacrifices the animal instead of Isaac.

The rabbi related this portion to my life, saying that God was testing me the way that he had tested Abraham, and that I should never abandon God no matter what my travails.

My mother made the most of the occasion. Afterward, she served herring, cake and whatever she could find to try to make this as much a celebration as possible.

My dream was to have a bicycle. I had been begging for one for a long time. However, much of our money, what little there was, had to go toward the purchase of food and necessities for my father like sweaters, socks and bread — otherwise he would freeze or starve — and toward our own meager upkeep. Still, my mother managed to present me with a bicycle as a bar mitzvah present, and I was over the moon with joy. This gave me some desperately needed fun and freedom to roam the Riviera.

Shortly after, I received a letter of congratulations from my father. But he also wrote to my mother, expressing his sadness at missing the bar mitzvah, which coincided with their 14th wedding anniversary.

"I don't need to tell you how much I love you … continue to keep me in your heart," he wrote. "May God give that we can start a new life once the war is over.… I cannot express in words how much I love you."

We received another letter, dated November 11, 1941, in which he wrote to thank us for a package that we had managed to send.

"I can honestly say the content amazed me," he wrote. "Everything was in good condition and I sat down to a breakfast I haven't had in 1.5 years. It was the first time since (Fresnay camp) I had bread with butter."

In another letter, he writes to thank us for the socks that we sent. He said his shoes were wearing out, and the entire camp was up to its knees in mud.

I enrolled in a local elementary school, but I didn't speak much French and didn't understand what was going on in class. It was incredibly boring to sit for hours on end in a classroom without understanding what was going on, so I ended up playing hooky a lot. I would go to the movies, paying for tickets with money I earned on the black market, or sometimes just sneaking in through the back door. I remember seeing "Zorro." That was one of my favorite movies. I also remember "Les Cinq Sous de Lavarede" or "The Five Cents of Lavarede," a very popular movie at the time. Incidentally, the composer of

the film's score, Polish-born French composer Casimir
Oberfeld, was deported to Auschwitz and died there in
1945.

View of Gurs internment camp from the camp
water tower. My father was incarcerated here until
his deportation to Auschwitz. (Courtesy of the
United States Holocaust Memorial Museum)

I was enrolled in a French elementary school after my mother and I escaped to Nice in 1941. (I am in the third row from the bottom, last boy on the right.)

I had made friends with other kids, some from school and others on the street, whose families had farms outside of town. These were essential connections to get food: cauliflower, broccoli, turnips. Food was always in short supply so it was very precious. The government issued food ration cards; but Jews who signed up for them had to submit their addresses, unwittingly giving up their location to the Nazis. We did not have ration cards. It fell largely to me to obtain food, and luckily, I was able to buy it cheaply through my farm connections and then sell it on the black market. I pocketed quite a bit of money by selling vegetables. I also dealt in cigarettes.

NO REPLY

My little business not only enabled me to buy movie tickets, but I also developed a side business, trading in stamps. I would line up at the post office as soon as a new issue of stamps would come out and buy whole blocks of them. Then I would go to the park on Sunday, when the stamp collectors gathered, to sell them. One such stamp that I have kept to this day has the image of Hitler and was issued on April 20, 1937, to commemorate his birthday. (In later years, I tried to sell the Hitler stamps, but they aren't worth much!)

Stamps issued to commemorate Hitler's birthday. I loved to collect stamps and traded them on the black market as a way to earn money for our survival.

Pamela Sampson

I often went to hotels on the Riviera to sell my vegetables. One such venue was the high-end Hotel Continental, where Jews with financial resources stayed. The doorman at the hotel would announce, "Heinz is here and he wants to come up!" I would then knock on the doors of the various hotel rooms, and sell my vegetables. I did the same at the Hotel Negresco. The Mautner family, the cosmetics wholesaler for whom my father had once sold cosmetics, was staying there and I sold food to them.

So with the help of my bicycle, I was very active on the black market and spent much of my adolescence on the street, selling illicit goods.

The storm clouds continued to gather. On January 20, 1942 — a date forever to be etched as one of the darkest on the crowded calender of Jewish tragedy — high-ranking officials from Nazi Germany met in the Berlin suburb of Wannsee to discuss and coordinate the "Final Solution" to the Jewish question. Hitler had already decided on the mass murder of Jews at some point in 1941. But its coordination hadn't been mapped out until Reinhard Heydrich, a top Nazi in charge of the Gestapo and other organizations that terrorized Germany's enemies, convened the Wannsee Conference.

The Vichy regime's cooperation with the Nazis made it easy to implement the Final Solution in France. Jews were required to register and disclose their addresses to authorities, and when the time came for roundups, the

NO REPLY

French police participated without fail. Jewish deportations from France began in March 1942. That year, more than 40 trains carrying Jewish men, women and children left French territory headed for Auschwitz.

My mother and I were lucky to have left Paris. On July 16-17, 1942, the French police launched "Operation Spring Breeze," rounding up more than 13,000 Jews, including 4,000 children. They were locked in the "Vélodrome d'Hiver" bicycle stadium without food or other assistance, or were taken to other internment camps, and then deported.

But we were far from safe. To meet Nazi deportation quotas, German, Austrian and Polish Jews were arrested en masse in southern France and handed over to the Germans. The French also began turning over foreign Jews being held in camps like Gurs.

In Nice, French police were picking Jews straight off of the Riviera's famed Promenade des Anglais, a luminous walkway bordering the Mediterranean. Lined with cafés and art deco hotels like the Negresco, the Promenade was a beautiful place to stroll — unless your identification papers marked you as a Jew.

It was the end of the summer of 1942, and we were in a life-and-death situation; at any minute, we could face arrest.

We had to go into hiding immediately. Luckily, my mother had made the acquaintance of a non-Jewish family, and we were given hiding space their attic. (I assume we paid them, but I am not sure.) We had to move so quickly that we didn't have time to go back to our hotel to get our few remaining possessions, including a suitcase and clothing. We hid with only the clothes we were wearing that day.

Two other Jewish families hid with us: one family including a furrier named Merkel; and a woman and her daughter. The woman had known the furrier for some time; he had sewn her diamonds into the shoulder pad of her fur coat to hide them.

But one day, when she went to retrieve the diamonds in order to buy false papers, the diamonds were missing. Of course, she couldn't go to the police or we'd all be arrested. Pure and simple, Merkel had stolen the diamonds. It caused a huge drama in that small attic. I don't know if the woman and her daughter survived the war, but if they didn't, it wouldn't be too far-fetched to blame their deaths on the missing diamonds. After the war, I learned that Merkel settled in Chicago.

We were holed up in the attic for two weeks, during which time I only left once: to sneak back to Hotel Rambaldi to get our last belongings so that I could sell them. We needed the money to buy false ID cards. Was I afraid? My emotions in detail I do not recall, but I wasn't so afraid that I couldn't undertake this task. Anyway, I was kind of a daredevil. I took those possessions to a local auction establishment and sold them for what money I could get.

Once again, my mother's ability to clandestinely network was absolutely critical in saving our lives. She had become acquainted with a young man who went by the name of "Fred Roy," although his real name was Manfred Rosenthal. He was a Jew from Berlin, a guy in his 20s, unmarried and a schemer type, a man for all seasons. He dealt in false identification papers, bribed police and somehow obtained or stole blank ID cards. My mother gave him 10,000 French francs, and he sold us ID papers that identified us as Christians. Armed with those papers, my mother and I left the attic in the middle of the night to meet a smuggler who took us to Annemasse, a city very close to the Swiss border.

Of all the trains and ships we had boarded to try to escape the Nazis, this car drive was perhaps the most perilous trip of all. The screws were getting tighter and tighter. Everyone understood that Jews who were taken into custody were shipped to unknown destinations, places no one wanted to go.

As we approached Annemasse, a member of the French Milice forced our driver to stop. We were terrified. The Milice was an extremist paramilitary force serving under the Vichy regime that hunted down members of the French Resistance and helped arrest Jews.

The man seemed to sense that our papers were false, and he questioned my mother in French.

"Excusez-moi, madame. Ce sont vos papiers?" ("Excuse me, Madame, are these your papers?")

In French, my mother replied, "Bien sûr." ("Of course.")

Sarcastically, he responded, "Si vous êtes sur, je vais vous laisser passer." ("If you are sure, I'll let you go.") Inexplicably, he allowed us to proceed. We were extremely lucky. Many other Jews were caught before reaching Switzerland and arrested.

The driver dropped us off at the foot of the mountain near the border and told us, "If you walk 1,000 meters, you will come to the border."

There were huts all along the border where the Swiss police stayed. Our smuggler alerted us to the fact that the border police usually went inside their huts when it rained. At that moment, luckily, it happened to be raining hard. We saw no police. We walked and walked for three, maybe four hours.

Suddenly, we heard the clicking of a rifle, and someone behind us shouted, "Arretez! Vous etes en Suisse!" ("Stop! You are in Switzerland!")

These were the words that we had been desperate to hear. We could only hope these words meant we were safe.

CHAPTER 5

WE HAD FLED Berlin with barely a suitcase, crisscrossed the Atlantic, run the entire length of France. It had been a long, weary and almost surreal trial for a child. Finally, after sloshing in the darkness through miles of mud, my mother and I crossed the finish line that separated life from death. On a dark night in September 1942, we made it to Switzerland, a neutral country surrounded on all sides by Nazi or Axis troops. The Germans would occupy southern France just two months later.

Four years of running, and yet we weren't far from our starting point, and barely a train trip to the nearest death camp. It had been a chaotic, 8,000-mile journey that intensified in terror with each passing month. We had lost everything, and our family had scattered far and wide in a desperate bid for safety.

Far worse than anything else was the unknown fate of my father. We had no idea where he was and whether he was still alive. The Hangman was hunting Jews down every European street and alley, in every building and under every floorboard. By some miracle of luck or fate,

Mutti and I had evaded the noose awaiting us, but what about Papi?

My mother and I spent our first night in Switzerland in a soccer dugout that had been converted into a holding place for refugees who managed to get across the border.

From there we were brought to a village in the vicinity of Bern called Eriswil, where we stayed in barracks maintained by the Swiss Army. Men and women were separated but ate meals together. The food was simple and adequate. I found other kids to play with. In the days and weeks to come, I helped in a local bakery, which became my first experience in what was to become my profession in the years ahead.

A Swiss sergeant named Karl Oesch took me under his wing. At Christmas, he even took me to Bern to spend time with his family.

The hardest part for me was being separated from my mother. I became a ward of the Swiss Child Relief Organization, which placed me with a Swiss Jewish family named the Goetschels. I was allowed to see my mother only once every six weeks. This was the Swiss government policy.

I spent 18 months with the Goetschels and their two sons, Pierre and Jean, who were just a little older than me. I will forever remember the way they embraced me and treated me as one of their own. Mr. Goetschel owned four silk stores that sold ties, fabric, scarves and other items. He was very successful and even knew the Aga Khan personally.

Mrs. Goetschel would sit with me in the evenings to tutor me. She literally spent hours every night trying to help me catch up with school work since I had been out of school for not just two years but actually four years, if you count the two years I spent on the streets of France selling stamps, vegetables and cigarettes and going to the movies instead of going to school. I was far behind in all academic areas, and Mrs. Goetschel was determined to get me to my correct scholastic level. We stayed up very late at night working on reading, writing and math. I even had to learn the language, since Swiss German is very distinct from the standard German that I spoke. She was a very rare woman.

Like the Goetschel boys, I became a boy scout and learned gardening, went on field trips and participated in all sorts of scouting activities. I also participated in the rituals of family life, which were not without significant influence.

In the 1940s, people young and old alike smoked with abandon, though the young did it secretly. But the Goetschels had a philosophy that, rather than have their children smoke in secret, they preferred to have them smoke out in the open, in a way that allowed the parents to supervise.

So the routine was one that I have not forgotten to this day. We would sit in the living room on Saturday nights, listening to classical music. Each boy was given one cigarette. As we listened to Mozart, Haydn, or Bach on their phonograph, we would smoke. This was a ritual that I came to appreciate and looked forward to. In addition to this, Mrs. Goetschel always managed to acquire some chocolate and would hand each of us boys a piece in a way that made it like a ceremony.

Mr. Goetschel had a huge map of Europe on the wall and would move little flags around the map that denoted the movements of the German Army. I remember the little flags showing the Wehrmacht during the Battle of Stalingrad in 1942-43. It was a critical turning point in the war on the Eastern Front, with the Russians successfully fending off the German attack. I remember the little flags being moved as the Wehrmacht retreated.

We also monitored the progress of the war on the radio via German language broadcasts. Of course, the Germans never admitted that they were falling back; instead they talked about repositioning their forces for tactical reasons.

The war had halted the tourist industry in Switzerland, so famed resorts like St. Moritz and Lugano were empty. The government requisitioned these resorts to house refugees, emptying them of the fine furnishings and leaving only the barest of essentials. My mother was sent to one of these places in Lucerne. She had quite a bit of freedom while she was there and was able to go into town on occasion.

NO REPLY

A camp near the hotel housed Allied fliers shot down in bombing raids over Germany. That meant there were not only foreign Jews in Switzerland, but also German defectors, Russian prisoners of war who had escaped from Germany, and many others. It was like the movie "Casablanca," a mecca of displaced people.

My mother kept looking for my father and other family members. She sent a letter to Uncle Erwin, my father's brother, who was trapped in Berlin with his wife, and received a reply on September 30, 1942.

The Gestapo censored the mail out of Germany, so Erwin had to be very careful in what he wrote. In a cryptic postcard, he wrote that my elderly grandmother Eugenie "had to leave 14 days ago." These strange and vague words had a sinister meaning: she had been deported. My grandfather, Saly, had passed away years before the war; elderly Eugenie was deported all alone. Erwin noted that at least she had had "a happy moment" when she received mail from Palestine, confirming that both my Uncle Walter and my cousin Liesl, Erwin's daughter, were safe.

Erwin also wrote that he and his wife were "working very hard." This is how we understood that they were being used as slave laborers. At that time, Germany was using forced labor to support its war effort, so my aunt and uncle may have been working in a factory, although I don't know whether it was making armaments or helmets or what. To this postcard, he added these ominous words: "Our little circle is always getting smaller." Years later, we would understand that this meant the deportation of our friends and family.

The postcard sent by Uncle Erwin in Berlin to my mother in Switzerland in 1942. We would never hear from him again.

My mother heard a rumor that led her to believe my father had been sent to a city in Poland called Lodz, the location of the second-largest ghetto after Warsaw. Jews had been forced to resettle in these ghettos, which were sealed off from the rest of the world, making it easy for the Nazis to use them for forced labor and to rob and starve them, and to deport whomever was left to death camps.

NO REPLY

My mother sent a postcard addressed simply to "Hermann Goldstein, Lodz, Poland," on August 11, 1943.

"My dear Hermann ... I am together with Heinz and we, thank God, are in good health. We hope the same for you. Regards and kisses, Yours, Rita." The postcard came back. There was no reply.

Following 18 months with the Goetschels, I was moved to another family. I believe this was in early 1944, and the war had turned definitively in favor of the Allies.

This was a non-Jewish family, the Wernlis, who lived in the small village of Grenchen at the foot of the Jura Mountains, just north of Bern. Mr. Wernlis was a secondary school teacher. Mrs. Wernlis was a housewife. They had two daughters, one about 20 years old and an older daughter, who was married with a baby. I appreciated that they never attempted to convert me to Christianity. In fact, they sent me every Sunday to a Hebrew school in Basel. It was about 15 minutes by train. They said I deserved to be with my own kind, and I enjoyed these hours that I spent learning Hebrew.

This couple had never been in contact with Jews before, and so they asked to see my penis: they wanted to see what a circumcision looked like! I was taken aback by this request — by this time I was 15 years old and not anxious to drop my pants in front of complete strangers, but I hinted that I would leave the door open while I showered so they could have a peek.

Pamela Sampson

From there, the Swiss Red Cross assigned me to the Ecole d'Humanité, a progressive boarding school founded by the German visionary educator Paul Geheeb, who had been forced to flee the Nazis. Geheeb was closely acquainted with the Nobel Prize-winning Indian poet Rabindranath Tagore. Most students at the school were refugees of one sort or another, including Jewish children.

The school was located in a chalet at the foot of the Swiss Alps; thus there was plenty of time for skiing and hiking. Classes were small, and the education focused on the classics: there were pictures of Beethoven, Mozart, Brahms all over the place. The dormitory was co-ed, which was very unusual at the time. It was run on democratic principles, with the student body deciding a certain number of matters, including the scholastic itinerary. It was really like a commune of youngsters with everyone assigned responsibilities. I was put to work in the kitchen. That's what got me hooked on cooking.

I made a lot of friends, including Hans von Brauchitsch. He was a nephew of Walther von Brauchitsch, the commander-in-chief of the Germany Army until 1941. I knew he was German, and I was puzzled as to why he was at the school. Decades later, I learned that he had settled in California, so I called him for a chat. That was when he told he that his mother had been Jewish, and that Hitler had allowed the family to leave Germany.

NO REPLY

I developed a love for the kitchen at Ecole d'Humanite, and it was decided — I don't know by whom — that I should attend the Swiss Hotel School in Luzerne.

The fees for the school were paid by a prominent Jewish family whose name was Benedict. My family had done business with them before the war. The Benedicts owned four department stores called "Innovatione" and lived in a beautiful home near the top of a mountain in the Italian part of Switzerland.

I attended the Swiss Hotel School and was given intensive training in both cooking and service. The school was half-hotel and half-school, kind of a work-study program. It was real training in French haute cuisine, as developed by the great chef Auguste Escoffier. It was he, I believe, who separated the French restaurant kitchen into stations, where cooks were assigned to prepare only one specific type of food and thus excel at its preparation. We learned about the complex hierarchy that made up the kitchen — all under the command of the chef and his second-in-command, the sous-chef.

First was the cold kitchen, primarily for cold appetizers like caviar and shrimp. Here I would do things such as remove lobsters from the shell, sauté them with paprika and butter, douse them with dry sherry and then ladle them with bechamel, a white cream sauce made with melted butter and flour and milk. Then they would be browned under a broiler. There was cooking involved, but it was still called the "cold kitchen."

The sauce station of course was for the main French sauces like bechamel and hollandaise. Then there was the fry cook, known as the entremetier, for any food needing to be deep-fried in boiling oil. There was the roast station for beef, turkey, Cornish hen and the like. And of course, there was the pastry station.

We rotated among these stations and also learned the operation of a restaurant.

The Swiss Hotel School was not a boarding school, and so I was assigned to live with two different Orthodox Jewish families in Lucerne. I spent a year or less with each family, and was obliged to participate in strict religious observance. This meant eating kosher food, praying daily, attending synagogue and observing the Sabbath.

Then, one day in May 1945, without any fanfare that I can recall, the war in Europe was over. I don't have any firm memory of learning the Germans had surrendered, or that Hitler was dead. We had been expecting an Allied victory; the key question was, would it come in time to save my father?

Much of Europe lay in ruins. Switzerland, however, emerged largely unscathed, and while there still weren't regular tourists, it became the rest-and-relaxation destination for American GIs stationed in post-war Europe. They fascinated me and made a deep impression on everyone.

NO REPLY

The first thing that came to my attention was a particular dining habit. When we served apple pie, the GIs would scoop out and eat the fruit filling, leaving the crust on the plate. This created a scandal among us students. In Europe, it was considered good manners to eat everything on your plate, especially with the hunger that so many millions of people experienced across the continent during the war.

Eventually, I found a job decorating cakes at a bakery in Lucerne and moved in with my mother, who was still at the hotel. I would go to my job during the day and spend hours making pastry dough. At night, I would take a cable car down the mountain and go look for the GIs. They always knew where the fun was. They mostly headed to nightclubs in the evening, and so I tagged along. It was typical in 1946. The world was healing, and in the process seizing every opportunity for fun.

At one of the clubs I learned the jitterbug, which the Nazis had banned as decadently American. I also developed an appreciation for big band music like the legendary Glenn Miller's "In the Mood," which epitomized the American swing era. I became friendly with some of the GIs and took them shopping. Cuckoo clocks were the one thing they would buy without exception. I would take them to certain watch repair shops that sold cuckoo clocks and be paid a commission by the shop. That is how I earned much of my spending money.

Pamela Sampson

Like the rest of the world, I was fascinated with America. People paid a premium to get hold of anything American — a Parker 51 fountain pen, an army-issued raincoat, a carton of Chesterfields, chewing gum. The GIs were worshipped. A GI who might have been a lowly dishwasher from Texas, for example, would be revered in post-war Europe like a celebrity. Everyone admired how casual the GIs were, how totally uninhibited they seemed in their outward behavior: totally un-British, with no inkling of formality; and so unlike the intellectual, snobby French. The lighthearted, let-loose spirit appealed to everyone. The GIs oozed with charisma and, of course, had immense chances with the opposite sex.

Everything was chaotic and upside down just after the war. There was a Missing Persons Bureau, but we were able to find nothing out about my father. My mother had sent out letters, like trial balloons, to various addresses trying to locate him, but received no reply.

After the war, Switzerland came under intense criticism for some of its actions, including its trade and financial dealings with Germany, and also for turning away roughly 30,000 desperate Jews who had tried to enter. I can only speak for myself. I encountered not a single incident of anti-Semitism in Switzerland. I was protected, fed, housed, and educated for five years. The country saved me, my mother and 20,000 other Jews. For that, I will remember the Swiss with nothing but total gratitude.

My mother and I in Switzerland at the end of the war.

Finally, in 1947, our visas for the U.S. were approved — but just for two of us, my mother and me. What about my father? This tortured us. I was maybe 11 years old the last time that I saw him. Now we were leaving Europe for America, and I was 19.

We wanted to get to America badly, where we had relatives. Lother, my father's brother, had arrived in Philadelphia a couple of years before Kristallnacht, when it was still possible to get a fairly quick visa for America. My mother's sister, Berta, who had had the great fortune of reaching Cuba with her family just weeks before we left on the St. Louis, had also made it to America.

CHAPTER 6

ON A RAW and wintry day in February 1947, the former warship SS America pulled into New York harbor with us on board. Lother was there to meet us. My mother's step-brother, Morris Lewin, was also there. He had come to the United States in 1928, but didn't like it and returned to Germany. After Hitler rose to power, Uncle Morris was able to return to the U.S. in 1938.

As for me, I was so excited by our arrival in New York and all that it implied.

As we started out in America, my mother and I were in the care of Jewish welfare organizations like the Joint, which had played such a crucial role during the St. Louis drama, and the Hebrew Immigrant Aid Society. For our first few weeks, we were lodged with an American-Jewish family. They didn't ask us about our experiences. They seemed complete-ly detached from the enormous suffering that we European Jews had endured. They didn't want to know. That was how it was back then, complete silence around our persecution. Survivors tried not to think about what had happened to them because no one wanted to know.

Pamela Sampson

My mother set to work immediately. She had taken a chocolate-making course shortly before we left Germany, and she and Morris' wife began manufacturing chocolates in a loft on 47th Street in Manhattan. They called the store "Lemore," a play on Morris Lewin's name.

My mother also worked as a waitress, and in hotels as a chambermaid. It was certainly a step down from life in Germany, but she was very driven to make a life for herself in America.

Even though we found employment quickly, I remember we were called "refugees" for the longest time, which I didn't like, because there was a stigma attached to being a refugee in those days. You were like a displaced person, a person without roots or stability; a person with nothing, who belonged nowhere. Most of us refugees were in one form or another Holocaust survivors. We gathered at the Senator Cafeteria on 96th Street. Refugees would lounge and socialize there, drinking endless coffee. I had many friends who were survivors — some with tattoos showing they had been in Auschwitz. They didn't talk about their experiences; some things were just too awful to verbalize.

Yet knowledge of what the Jews of Europe had faced was being made public. Newsreels in theaters across the country — the way Americans received much of their news during World War II — showed motion picture footage taken by the U.S. Army of liberated Nazi concentration camps. General Dwight Eisenhower had ordered such documentation so there would be lasting proof of the unimaginable

70

persecution that had taken place. Footage of survivors who were barely more than skeletons, of twisted bodies heaped into piles, of crematoria ovens with human bones visible inside, provoked not just revulsion but widespread sympathy, which had been so lacking before the war.

Having received hospitality training in Switzerland was a stroke of good fortune for me. I spoke only limited English (I had learned some in the Ecole d'Humanite and had practiced speaking with the GIs) and yet I was never without a job. I had the choice, literally, of dozens of places to work.

Eventually, I was hired at the upscale Park Sheraton, just across the street from Carnegie Hall. I walked in and introduced myself to the general manager, explaining in great detail my training at the Swiss Hotel School. Unimpressed, he turned to his assistant manager and said, "Tell him how you started here."

So the assistant manager explained that he had started out as an elevator operator. In those days, elevators were manually operated, requiring someone to stand there and make sure the elevator stopped at the correct floor. All new employees were expected to start as elevator operators, and if one excelled, one could be promoted to bellhop.

I operated the elevator between floors 26 and 31. These floors housed elegantly appointed suites where permanent residents like Mae West, Tommy Dorsey and Eleanor Roosevelt lived.

Mrs. Roosevelt rode my cab on a daily basis. Yet I never mentioned the war or got personal with her. This was something you did not do: you never addressed the guests. I never mentioned that I was one of the passengers on the MS St. Louis; I never mentioned FDR's failure to grant refuge to the passengers; I never mentioned the years of running and hiding and barely escaping with my life. I never mentioned my father. Where was he? What had happened to him? A decade after last seeing him, we still didn't know for sure.

I was angry; I wanted revenge, and working in the Park Sheraton's elevator was unsatisfying, to say the least. I enlisted in the Air Force, imagining that I would be sent to Germany, perhaps as an interpreter, with some kind of authority. But they made me a clerk typist, and I was stationed at a base in Cheyenne, Wyoming. There, I had disturbing experiences.

My papers arrived before me, and so it became evident to the squadron that a Jew was joining. There weren't many of us, and I made friends of course, but there was always someone who hated Jews with a passion. Once, I went on leave to North Dakota and stopped at a roadside bar. I tried to order a drink but the bartender refused to serve me. He insisted I wasn't 21 years old. I told him that I could prove my age with citizenship papers. His response: "Get the hell out of here." Did he know I was Jewish? I didn't look like the average North Dakotan and that was enough to get me booted out of a bar. After a year, I was honorably discharged. It wasn't for me.

Years later, I did go back to Germany and sought out the place where I had spent my early years. I knocked on the door of our former apartment on the Clausewitzstrasse in Berlin. A woman whom I did not recognize answered the door and went stone-like when I introduced myself. A Jew has returned? She probably thought I was going to try to reclaim the apartment, but I just wanted to see it. With wariness in her eyes, she allowed me in.

It didn't matter. New York was the place for me. I was an impatient young man who wanted a job using my kitchen skills. I thought this would bring me the most success in the least amount of time. I found work in the kitchens of a number of high-end resorts: the Astor Hotel, the New Yorker, the St. Moritz on Central Park West and others. I was making somewhat of a name for myself, so when word went out that the ultra-exclusive Greenbrier Hotel in West Virginia was looking for some experienced help, I was recommended and hired, sight unseen.

The Greenbrier, set on thousands of verdant acres in White Sulphur Springs, was a vacation playground for the elite. President Woodrow Wilson and other American presidents routinely stayed there; its golf course was one of the best. I was sent to the personnel office as soon as I arrived and started to fill out the paperwork. A young woman was there to assist me, but as soon as she saw my application, she warned me.

"I shouldn't be telling you this," she said, "but with that name, you will last here two weeks."

The name "Goldstein" was a dead giveaway that I was Jewish. The resort would not accept Jewish guests or employees, and Jewish-sounding names were an easy way to ferret them out. The staff, meanwhile, was full of Germans and listed as clients suspected Nazi sympathizers like the Duke and Duchess of Windsor.

I was taken aback. Anti-Semitism in America? This was a huge shock to me.

I had to come up with a Christian-sounding name on the Greenbrier application. I thought about a last name starting with "G" and the name Garland occurred to me, since I had such admiration for Judy Garland. However, by the time the name ended up on the application, it came out as "G-A-L-L-A-N-T." But at least I was hired as assistant sauce cook.

Everyone working in the kitchen, from the executive chef to the pastry cook, figured out I was Jewish. They were all Swiss, while the waiters were mostly German. The Greenbrier accepted black employees, although they were limited to peeling potatoes and washing dishes.

Segregation was endemic across the southern U.S. It was normal to see "Whites Only" signs on bathrooms and other public places. Blacks, who were exploited at every turn, were made to sit in the backs of buses; seats up front were for white people. True to form, employee accommodations at the Greenbrier were separated by color, in different buildings.

The Greenbrier was a seasonal job, though, and soon I was back in New York, working at the Dellwood Country

Club. A chef by the name of Henry Haller, who was originally from Switzerland, hired me. Officially, I was the fry cook, but in actuality I was Haller's assistant sous-chef, since there were only two of us in the kitchen. This was in the mid-1950s. Some years later, Haller rose to fame within the profession after he was chosen by President Lyndon B. Johnson to work as the White House chef.

Back to my troublesome name: I changed it once and for all after another incident.

Pan Am Airways was advertising for stewards between the ages of 21 and 35 who spoke at least two languages and had culinary and hospitality training. I spoke French, German and English and met every qualification that the airline was seeking. I even had served briefly in the Air Force. So I answered the advertisement feeling confident that I had a real shot at the job. I was so excited.

At the time, I had been going informally by the name of Henry Gallant, but for my interview with Pan Am, I disclosed that my real name was Goldstein. I felt that I had to do this because if I landed the job, I would have to get a passport. It was exactly at that point during the interview that things turned sour.

I remember almost verbatim the rejection letter I got ("It is the opinion of this board that your qualifications are not best suited for the position"). It really stung because I knew that wasn't true. The problem was that I was Jewish.

Thus on January 29, 1958, I legally changed my name so as to be known officially and forever as Henry Gallant, and leaving a certain amount of troubles behind. It didn't seem like a big deal; I was simply doing what some others were doing. Hollywood was full of Jewish actors who had changed their names to increase their appeal or help their careers: Emanuel Goldenberg became Edward G. Robinson; Jacob Julius Garfinkel became John Garfield; Betty Perske transformed into Lauren Bacall.

Well, my mother threw a fit. She felt that my father's name was the only thing, and the most valuable thing, that he had been able to leave me. Indeed, there were a few prominent Goldsteins here and there. Ruby Goldstein was a popular boxing referee and Nathaniel Goldstein was attorney general of New York, both stood as proof to my mother that the Goldstein name was fine the way it was.

"If they didn't have to change their names, why should you?" she insisted.

But I never experienced another job rejection after that.

I traveled extensively for work and for play. At one point, I went to Montreal for a three-day vacation. There, I happened to notice a young woman in front of a shoe store, waiting for a bus. She was very attractive, tall with honey-colored hair, azure eyes. I was on my way to a nightclub. I wanted to introduce myself to her, so I asked her for some directions in French. She answered that she didn't speak French. I detected a distinct German accent, and I said, "In that case, I can ask you the same question in German."

Next thing I knew, we were seated at a café, having coffee and cake. Her name was Ilse Oberpaul.

Ilse was born in 1934 in a small German town called Ludwigshafen am Rhein, near Mannheim. Her father was a border control officer and her mother, a housewife. When the war erupted, the family was put on a truck in the middle of the night and eventually moved to Munich. At some point, her father was sent to serve in a tank battalion and was captured by the Russians somewhere on the Eastern Front and, along with scores of other German POWs, forced to march on foot back to Germany.

The Allies, meanwhile, began bombing the city in 1942 and intensified the attack through 1944 and 1945. Ilse was forced to spend days at a time with her mother and brother in the cellar to try to avoid being killed. The family's home was bombed twice; the second time, they were buried in rubble and it took nearly 48 hours to get them out. Ilse was only about 8 or 9 years old at the time and had been so frightened that she bit through her tongue and couldn't open her mouth; they had to cut through her upper lip to unclench her jaw. Ironically, she sustained more physical injuries than me during the war.

Another twist in her saga was the discrimination she faced in Munich, which is situated in majority-Catholic Bavaria. Hunger was rampant in Germany after the war, and word got around that Catholic churches were distributing potatoes. Once a week, she would stand in line at the local Catholic parish to get potatoes. But then it was discovered that she was Lutheran, and no more potatoes were forthcoming. The priest, a massive holy man whom Ilse said reminded her of a slimy fat frog, held her hand and squeezed it, telling her: "If you convert, you can have potatoes."

To escape the lingering fascist mindset of post-war Germany, Ilse found a job through a Canadian government advertisement. She left for Canada at age 18 and ended up as a domestic servant for a Montreal hospital executive and his wife. She worked from 6 a.m. to 11 p.m. six days a week for $35 a month, with more than half of her salary going to the government to repay her passage from Europe. Ilse did everything from cooking and serving all meals, to cleaning the three-story mansion, to taking the entire charge of a spoiled 9-year-old girl, to ironing and starching the ruffles on the child's dresses. Canada likes to talk about its humanity, but it has a history that sometimes says otherwise.

Anyway, that's how Ilse and I met. We were instantly charmed by each other.

I had a problem, though. Ilse wasn't Jewish, and this was devastating to my mother. Luckily, Ilse was very interested in Judaism and converted after several years of instruction (and a few thousands dollars in donations to the rabbi). In 1961, Ilse and I were married. Our son, Mark, was born on April 11, 1963.

Our wedding day in Las Vegas in 1961.

The year 1961 was a big year for me in another way. Since arriving in the United States, I had literally held dozens of jobs, including stints in Florida and the Catskills. This was the year that I finally found my true niche in the supper club circuit.

I heard through the New York hotel grapevine that the Waldorf Astoria's famed Empire Room — shut down by its owners two years before due to union issues — was opening again.

The Empire Room was in the top echelon of the New York supper clubs. It had a polished dance floor, a tuxedo-clad orchestra, sumptuous chandeliers, velvet drapes — the works. It drew the hottest acts and served great food. Benny Goodman, Edith Piaf and Cole Porter had graced its stage, and news of its reopening spread fast. I wanted to work there, and by a stroke of luck, I happen to know the new maître d'. He hired me as a waiter, and within three days, I was promoted to service captain.

We had to show up for work at 5 p.m., dressed in black tie, and get the dining room ready. Electricity filled the air as the young couples glowing in the beauty of youth and privilege and decked in formal attire would swoosh into the club. The heavyweights were there to entertain them: Lena Horne, Peggy Lee, Ella Fitzgerald, Johnny Mathis, Carol Channing, Steve Lawrence and Eydie Gorme, Muhammad Ali.

Of course, there was money in it for the employees. The cover charge was $15, and the food and alcohol were all high-end; the bill at the end of the night could easily top $100 for a table of two. I could make $300 to $500 a week in tips. That was big money in 1961.

Taking a punch from Muhammad Ali in
the Empire Room, circa 1965.

The tips were not the only thrill. Occasionally, a big name would walk in to see a show: Judy Garland, Frank Sinatra, Dustin Hoffman, Marlon Brando. The room glittered and not just because of the chandeliers.

Pamela Sampson

With Dolly Parton at the Empire Room, circa 1965.

We loved it when the Mafia showed up; they were effusive tippers. And they never came alone or in couples. They always brought the whole family: if one came, 20 would come. If the Genovese or Gambino clan showed up, they would take five or six tables and tip the maître d' very heavily to sit up front. In those days, a maître d' at the Empire Room could earn more than a doctor. Service captains like me didn't do badly, either. A mafia don would put $50 into my pocket and say, "Pick something out." And I would send over rounds of caviar, minute steaks or platters of shrimp.

NO REPLY

They seemed on the surface to be such generous and peaceful-minded souls, but then we'd read in the newspaper about a mob hit involving someone we had served a night or two before.

The fast-changing world of entertainment led to the demise of the Empire Room. It could no longer afford the salaries of the big entertainers, who originally earned $5,000 a week. Salaries eventually escalated to $10,000, then $15,000, then $20,000 and so on. Barbra Streisand was said to command $1 million for a live show. Stars like her could only play in Las Vegas, where the profit was made up at the gambling tables. The Empire Room couldn't really raise the cover charge of $15 without losing customers, and the audiences began to shrink, with only the top stars being able to draw a real crowd.

Rumors were constant that the room would close, and it did — along with other nightclubs like the St. Regis and the Persian Room of the Plaza.

I left for Atlanta, where I had been recruited to work in the Venetian Room nightclub of the Fairmont Hotel, in 1975.

Atlanta was called an international city, but back then it wasn't. It had maybe one Italian restaurant. If you wanted a bagel, you had to travel 20 miles. And it wasn't ready for the kind of leisure that the Fairmont was offering. Clients wondered what they would get for the $15 cover charge, and the answer of "a table and chair" dumbfounded people not used to high-end service. The

Venetian Room was transformed into a country music venue, which also failed, and eventually it became a banquet hall.

My next big professional step required my best European cooking skills and knowledge. My wife and I were members of Shearith Israel synagogue, and when the synagogue's caterer had a falling out with the rabbi, we took over his company. It was an exclusively kosher operation and was accredited to cater at all the synagogues. I bought it for $1,500 but really got nothing other than the name of the company, Prestige Caterers.

At that time, kosher food wasn't readily available the way it is today. Everything had to be made from scratch under the supervision of a mashgiah, who makes sure that all food preparation follows the strict laws of kashrut.

Within one year, sales soared — from $15,000 to $50,000. I assembled a crew of cooks and trained them. Our client list grew rapidly, thanks to word-of-mouth recommendations. Bar mitzvahs were a big business, as were traditional Jewish weddings.

In time, I wanted to branch out and really go for an expansion of the business. I started catering to non-Jewish events. One of my first big jobs was to cater a reception at the Centers for Disease Control, a big event marking the eradication of small pox.

A big setback came in 1994, when I had a heart attack. Ilse quit her job as a manager at Steak and Ale restaurant in order to help keep the company going. She became my right-hand man, so to speak, helping in all aspects of the business. Imagine this young German woman coming to America after the war and helping to operate one of the most successful kosher catering businesses in the Atlanta area!

Unfortunately I had another heart attack in 1998 and then three years later, we finally had to face the inevitable: we couldn't keep the company going, given my health and the changing tastes and demographics of Atlanta. After an incredibly successful run, Prestige Caterers closed on December 5, 2001.

Here I am with Ilse, my wife, and our son, Mark, on the occasion of his bar mitzvah in New York on April 11, 1976.

CHAPTER 7

As THE HORRORS of the Holocaust gradually emerged, it became clear that my father had not survived. Still, it wasn't until 1978, roughly 40 years after our fateful St. Louis voyage, that I received a letter from the International Tracing Service in Germany.

Dear Mr. Goldstein-Gallant,

Referring to your letter dated 24th October 1977 and to our acknowledgement of receipt of 8th November 1977 please be advised that a check of our records revealed the following information:

GOLDSTEIN Herman, born on 29th June 1889 in Herford; Citizenship: German; Religion: Jewish; was transferred from "Sammellager" (Assembly Camp) Drancy to Concentration Camp Auschwitz on 10th August 1942.

Unfortunately nothing is known to us with regard to the further fate of your father, but the possibility exists that your father also may have perished, a victim of the persecution.

NO REPLY

We regret very much to be unable to give you a fa-
vourable reply, and remain,
With kind regards,
A Opitz
Chief of Archives

We had known there was no hope of ever seeing my father alive, but now the Red Cross had made it official, putting it in writing.

We soon learned more details of my father's fate. French Nazi-hunter Serge Klarsfeld, whose father had died at Auschwitz, had spent years doing research and in 1978 issued a publication on the trains that deported Jews from France to their deaths in Nazi concentration camps.

From this we learned that my father had been on the first convoy of Jews from the unoccupied zone to be deported by the Vichy government. Convoy No. 17 held 525 women and 475 men, almost all of them German Jews. It left Gurs for Drancy on August 6, 1942. He was 53 years old.

Four days later, upon arrival at Auschwitz, 760 people were immediately gassed. More than 140 were tattooed with identification numbers. To the best of Klarsfeld's research, only one man from that convoy survived the war, and it was not my father. It is possible that my father succumbed before reaching the camp, having spent four days in a hot, sealed cattle car with no food or water;

however, it seems more likely that he was put to death in the gas chambers.

My mother had reason never to forgive the French. Here is their war record: one-quarter of all Jews in France under the Nazis were deported east to death camps.

View of Auschwitz-Birkenau concentration camp immediately after liberation in January 1945. (Courtesy of the United States Holocaust Memorial Museum)

Of the two branches of my family, no one was left in Germany. Those who hadn't fled were murdered.

Eugenie Goldstein, my German-born grandmother who was living in Berlin, was deported in September 1942 to Theresienstadt ghetto-camp outside of Prague, where many elderly Jews were sent. About 140,000 Jews were deported to Theresienstadt; most were later sent east to an extermination camp. My grandmother was among 33,000

Jews who died at Theresienstadt. Her death came on February 3, 1943, murdered at age 76 as an enemy of the Reich.

My Uncle Erwin Goldstein was deported with his wife, Margarete, on Transport No. 22 from Berlin on October 26, 1942. Their destination was Riga, Latvia, where firing squads were at work killing Jews. They were both 45 years old when they were deported and then shot to death. Their daughter, Liesl, had escaped with Uncle Walter to Palestine in the 1930s.

My Uncle Erwin and Aunt Margarete. They were deported from Berlin to Riga, Latvia, and shot to death in 1942.

Pamela Sampson

Decades after the St. Louis sailed, two researchers at the United States Holocaust Memorial Museum embarked on a mission. Scott Miller and Sarah A. Ogilvie, in their groundbreaking book, "Refuge Denied: The St. Louis Passengers and the Holocaust," traced the fate of every single passenger on board. Here is the breakdown, determined through painstaking research over a decade: 652 passengers survived; 255 were killed. All but one passenger sent to Britain survived; 87 passengers escaped Europe before the German invasion of Western Europe in May 1940. Of passengers sent to Belgium, Holland and France, 278 survived and 254 were murdered, including my father.

I have kept in touch with other St. Louis survivors. One theme that comes up again and again is how America's treatment of refugees has changed. Sometimes it is hard to see incidents like the Mariel boatlift.

In 1980, Cuban leader Fidel Castro — facing internal turmoil due to a weak economy — announced that anyone who could arrange transportation from the Mariel port in Cuba was free to leave. That prompted a massive exodus of Cubans who left for the United States.

Then-President Jimmy Carter let 125,000 Cuban refugees enter America — no questions asked. Nearly 1,700 boats arrived on American shores with for the most part penniless Cuban exiles. Among them were stealthily planted criminals and mental patients who had been released from jails and hospitals. Overnight, the Cuban population in Miami skyrocketed.

NO REPLY

Sometimes it's hard not to feel bitter. Cuba turned us away. America turned us away. My father and other family members were murdered. My childhood was aborted. Other families lost even more than I did.

Decades after the St. Louis voyage, the U.S. Senate passed a resolution recognizing June 9, 2009 as the 70th anniversary of the date when the St. Louis returned to Europe after its passengers were refused admittance to the United States.

Sponsored by Senator Herb Kohl, a Democrat from Wisconsin, the resolution honors the memory of the 937 refugees aboard the St. Louis and recognizes the anniversary "as an opportunity for public officials and educators to raise awareness about an important historical event the lessons of which are relevant to current and future generations."

When I think of future generations, my guess is that the experience of the Jews during World War II will become a religious thing, perhaps even more than a historical thing, maybe like the Haggadah, the story of Passover, which Jews recite over and over, every year. What we went through was big, and it seems to me that it will grow with the passage of time.

Yad Vashem, the museum in Israel dedicated to the memory of the victims of the Holocaust, has a program that recognizes the small number of non-Jews who — at great risk to themselves — helped rescue Jews during this terrible period. The museum bestows the honorary title of "Righteous Among the Nations" upon such rare heroes, which harkens the world not only to hail their acts of remarkable courage but also to recognize that action is possible, even in the face of the most savage evil.

On January 10, 1959, Captain Gustav Schroeder died. On March 11, 1993, he was posthumously granted the title of "Righteous Among the Nations." His captain's hat — with its blue and white flag surrounded by laurels, the emblem of the Hamburg-Amerika line — was donated to the United States Holocaust Memorial Museum.

Portrait of Gustav Schroeder, captain of the MS St. Louis. (Courtesy of the United States Holocaust Memorial Museum)

Afterword

IN THE DECADES since World War II, the voyage of the MS St. Louis has taken on significance far larger than the individual fates of its passengers. By belatedly stirring America's slumbering conscience, the tragedy of the St. Louis has provided momentum for a new and more compassionate immigration policy that does justice to the vision of the nation's Founding Fathers. The relaxation of restrictions has allowed the entry of scores of people fleeing persecution due to race, religion, nationality, membership in a particular social group, or political beliefs.

Some of that change came as early as the war's end, when President Harry Truman in December 1945 ordered immigration quotas to be filled by displaced persons, specifically seeking to help those Jews who survived the persecution. What a reversal from the days of abandonment, when Hermann, Rita and little Heinz Goldstein were left to fend for themselves on the dark eve of the Holocaust.

What has not changed since the 1939 voyage is that controversy still engulfs the subject of immigration. The demand for safe haven in the United States has exploded, and choosing whom to allow in has become a moral minefield. The United Nations counted in 2015 some 65 million people worldwide who had been displaced due to war and persecution, a figure that does not account for "climate migrants," people from countries whose natural environments are becoming unlivable due to pollution, overpopulation and other man-made harm. On top of these pressures is the threat of terrorism, which has increased suspicion of immigrants who might hold extremist ideologies.

Up to 200 million people could find themselves on the move by the middle of the 21st century, and odds are high that enormous numbers will try to push through U.S. gates. Where the choking point rests is a matter of conjecture; what is undeniable is that there is not enough room on American soil for everyone. It is legitimate to ask how much room is available for new citizens and their future descendants. For its survival, the United States must impartially evaluate each applicant who desires entry. This inevitably will lead to rejecting many.

Still, it is impossible not to see when looking in a mirror who we are: the product of generations of courageous and talented pioneers who came to America, building its sturdy pillars. Immigration is in our DNA: we are a biologically diverse people who have come together over the decades and centuries, sometimes peaceably and other times disagreeably, to forge a haven that has become the greatest force for liberty and democracy in history.

In these times of global conflict, overpopulation, environmental crisis and international terrorism, we must decide what we stand for. Is the Statue of Liberty still relevant? Does her torch still light the way to our shores? If yes, then we must take a lesson from the St. Louis episode. It's true that America cannot offer everything to everyone. But we — as a strong, free and compassionate people — certainly must offer more than no reply.

— Pamela Sampson, Atlanta, 2017

Henry Gallant with his granddaughter, Areanna.

Bibliography

Abella, Irving, and Harold Troper. None is Too Many: Canada and the Jews of Europe 1933-1948. New York: Random House, 1982.

Adler, Jacques. The Jews of Paris and the Final Solution: Communal Response and Internal Conflicts, 1940-1944. New York: Oxford University Press, 1987.

Bennett, Marion T., J.F. Findlay. American Immigration Policies. Washington: Public Affairs, 1963.

Browning, Christopher R., "From Humanitarian Relief to Holocaust Rescue: Tracy Strong Jr., Vichy Internment Camps, and the Maison des Roches in Le Chambon," Holocaust and Genocide Studies, Aug. 11, 2016.

Caron, Vicki. Uneasy Asylum: France and the Refugee Crisis 1933-1942. Stanford University Press, 1999.

Curtis, Michael. Verdict on Vichy: Power and Prejudice in the Vichy France Regime. New York: Arcade Publishing, 2002.

DeCoste, F.C., Bernard Schwartz, editors. The Holocaust's Ghost: Writings on Art, Politics, Law and Education. Edmonton: University of Alberta Press, 2000.

Duffy, Michael. "Iron Cross." FirstWorldWar.com. http://www.firstworldwar.com/atoz/ironcross.htm Aug. 22, 2009. Accessed August 2016.

Feingold, Henry L. The Politics of Rescue: The Roosevelt Administration and the Holocaust, 1938-1945. New Brunswick: Rutgers University Press, 1970.

Fortune Magazine, 15 Nov. 2015.

Friedlander, Saul. Nazi Germany and the Jews, Vol. 1: The Years of Persecution, 1933-1939. New York: HarperCollins, 1997.

Gellman, Irwin F. "The St. Louis Tragedy." American Jewish Historical Quarterly. December 1971.

Gilbert, Martin. The Holocaust: A History of the Jews of Europe During the Second World War. New York: Henry Holt, 1985.

Hapag-Lloyd AG. Shipping made in Hamburg: The history of the Hapag-Lloyd AG. Hamburg, Germany.

Hilberg, Raul. The Destruction of the European Jews. Holmes & Meier, 1985.

History.com, "Castro Announces Mariel Boatlift." This Day in History.

NO REPLY

http://www.history.com/this-day-in-history/
castro-announces-mariel-boatlift.
Accessed on Sept. 6, 2016.

Konovitch, Barry J. "The Fiftieth Anniversary of the St. Louis: What Really Happened." American Jewish History. Winter 1989-90.

Lambert, Raymond-Raoul. Diary of a Witness, 1940-1943. Librairie Artheme Fayard. 1985; Ivan R. Dee, 2007.

Levine, Robert M. Tropical Diaspora: The Jewish Experience in Cuba. University Press of Florida, 1993.

Marrus, Michael R., and Robert O. Paxton. Vichy France and the Jews. Stanford University Press, 1995.

Mendelsohn, John, and Donald S. Detwiler, editors. Jewish Emigration: The S.S. St. Louis Affair and Other Cases. Garland, 1982.

Newman, Ken. Swiss Wartime Work Camps: A Collection of Eyewitness Testimonies 1940-1945. Zurich: NZZ Verlag, 1999.

Ogilvie, Sarah A., and Scott Miller. Refuge Denied: The St. Louis Passengers and the Holocaust. Madison: University of Wisconsin Press, 2006.

Ryan, Donna F. The Holocaust & the Jews of Marseille. University of Illinois Press, 1996.

Thomas, Gordon, and Max Morgan Witts. Voyage of the Damned. New York: Skyhorse Publishing, 2010.

United States Holocaust Memorial Museum. "Editors Law." Timeline of Events. https://www.ushmm.org/learn/timeline-of-events/1933-1938/editors-law. Accessed on Aug. 1, 2016.

United States Holocaust Memorial Museum. "Antisemitic Legislation 1933-39." Holocaust Encyclopedia. https://www.ushmm.org/wlc/en/article.php?ModuleId=10007901. Accessed on Aug. 1, 2016.

United States Holocaust Memorial Museum. "Documents Required to Obtain a Visa." Holocaust Encyclopedia. https://www.ushmm.org/wlc/en/article.php?ModuleId=10007456. Accessed on Aug. 1, 2016.

United States Holocaust Memorial Museum, "United States Policy Toward Jewish Refugees, 1941-1952." Holocaust Encyclopedia. https://www.ushmm.org/wlc/en/article.php?ModuleId=10007094 Accessed on Oct. 20, 2016.

NO REPLY

Vincent, C. Paul. "The Voyage of the St. Louis Revisited."
Holocaust and Genocide Studies. Fall 2011.

Webster, Paul. Pétain's Crime: The Full Story of French
Collaboration During the Holocaust. London:
Macmillan, 1990.

Weinberg, Gerhard L. A World at Arms: A Global History
of World War II. Cambridge University Press, 1994.

Zuccotti, Susan. The Holocaust, the French, and the
Jews. New York: BasicBooks, 1993.

Made in the USA
Columbia, SC
14 May 2022

60407285R00071